BEYOND THE FRAME

What Art Taught Me About Business, Leadership & Life

Amol R.Kadam

DEDICATION

To my parents, Late Ramchandra & Ratnaprabha Kadam

Their presence has never faded. I lost my father before I could even step into adulthood, but the foundation they both built for me remained unshaken. As teachers, their upbringing shaped me long before I understood its depth, instilling in me the values of perseverance, curiosity, resilience, humility, grounding, and the calmness to navigate life's uncertainties.

After my father's passing, my mother's unconditional support became my strength. She encouraged my love for art and stood by me in my pursuit of a career in design, ensuring that I could continue my education despite the challenges. Her belief in me made all the difference.

This book is my attempt to reflect the qualities they both instilled in me — the ability to find happiness in yourself, the courage to embrace uncertainty, and the ability to see beyond the obvious. I carry their lessons with me every day, and I hope, in some way, this makes them proud.

TABLE OF CONTENT

INTRODUCTION

Let me start by saying … By no means am I writing this book to claim myself as a very successful artist. By no means am I a very successful businessman or a leader. In all three cases—art, business, and leadership—none of it was part of some grand strategy or a meticulously planned journey. I never set out to become a great artist or a great business leader. I simply embraced what came my way and did my best with whatever was thrown at me. Each step, each challenge, and each mistake shaped the path rather than the other way around.

This book is nothing but an attempt to document my thoughts as they came to my mind. It's not a prescription, a strategy, or a formula for success in art, business, or leadership. In fact, I can put my neck on the line and say that I haven't been a successful businessman, nor have I been an accomplished artist in any traditional sense. But I think it's about how I wanted each aspect of my life to be perfect, and at the same time, how I learned to embrace the imperfections, live with them, and still make the best out of every situation.

This book is simply my reflection on everything that goes through my mind when I think about art, business, and the many ways they intersect. I don't want to sound like a guru or a successful entrepreneur preaching to the world. This is not that kind of book. Instead, it's a deeply personal exploration of how art and business have shaped my journey and what I've learned along the way.

I have also curated specific art exercises for each of these concepts to help even non-artists explore them. These exercises are not about skill or technique; they are designed to encourage expression, break mental barriers, and allow anyone—regardless of their artistic background—to experience the transformative impact of creativity. Whether you pick up a brush, a pen, or just observe the world differently, the goal is to engage with art as a means of discovery and reflection.

REDISCOVERING ART AS MEDITATION

Growing up in India, I was always fascinated by art. As a child, I was naturally inclined toward drawing, painting, and creative expression. I was the go-to person in my school group for all science journal sketches, biology diagrams, and even Rangoli competitions. Art was my escape, my language. However, like many others in a society that prioritised engineering and medicine as the 'right' career paths, art was not considered a viable future. It was something you did if you weren't good at academics. But that wasn't my case—I was good at studies, and I had the option to pursue any mainstream career. Still, my heart was set on art. I rebelled against my parents, both teachers themselves, to allow me to join art school.

When I eventually entered the world of digital design, UX, and service design, my artistic roots faded into the background. The intensity of running a business, building a career, and managing the ups and downs of an entrepreneurial journey took over. I was constantly solving problems, designing experiences, and thinking strategically, but art—the act of creating for the sake of self-expression—became rare. I still carried a sketchbook during my travels, occasionally making sketches when inspiration struck, but it was inconsistent. Life had shifted towards deadlines, projects, and business growth. And with it came stress.

Stress, I realised, is something every entrepreneur faces. As my business grew, so did the weight of responsibility. The pressure to deliver, the constant decision-making, the unpredictability of running a company—it all built up over time. Headaches, fatigue, and mental exhaustion became a part of my daily life. It wasn't just about working hard; it was about carrying the emotional and mental load of leadership.

It was during one of these high-stress periods that I turned back to art—not as a profession, but as a personal escape. I found myself picking up my sketchbook more frequently, using art as a way to detach from the chaos. What started as a momentary distraction quickly became a powerful tool for mindfulness? I noticed how drawing, painting, and simply engaging with colours and textures calmed my mind. It felt like meditation, but in a way that suited my personality better. Unlike traditional meditation, where stillness and silence are emphasised, art allowed me to be engaged yet deeply relaxed. My mind was fully absorbed in the process, giving me a break from the constant noise of business challenges.

This connection between art and meditation became clearer to me as I explored it further. When you draw, your focus shifts entirely to the present moment. The strokes of a brush, the blending of colours, the movement of a pencil across paper—everything demands attention. You cannot think about past failures or future worries when you are deeply immersed in creating. This is exactly what mindfulness teaches, and art was giving me that same experience effortlessly.

Interestingly, my journey into rediscovering art also led me to explore art therapy. Not as a profession, but purely to understand how art impacts the mind. I pursued a certification in art therapy, not to teach others, but to deepen my own awareness of how creativity influences emotions, mental well-being, and stress levels. The more I learned, the more I realised t.hat art wasn't just a hobby—it was a powerful tool for mental clarity and healing.

Through this process, I also reflected on my personality. I have always been an introvert. Expressing myself through strong opinions or direct conversations wasn't my strength. But when it came to art, I never felt restricted. It allowed me to say things without words, to communicate emotions that I couldn't always verbalise. This was another reason why art worked so well as a meditative practice for me. It became a silent language, a way to process my thoughts and emotions without overthinking.

One of the most valuable lessons I learned from art—one that directly connects to business—is resilience. Art teaches you that mistakes are part of the process. A wrong stroke, an unbalanced composition, or an unexpected colour mix doesn't mean failure. It means adaptation. The same applies to entrepreneurship. I've made mistakes in my business—wrong decisions, misplaced trust, misjudged risks. But just like in art, those mistakes didn't mean the end; they meant learning. Over time, I became more patient, more accepting of the imperfections in both art and business.

Now, as I stand in front of large audiences at conferences, speaking about UX, service design, and business strategy, I often reflect on how much art has helped me reach this point. Coming from a Marathi vernacular medium school, English wasn't always natural to me. When I moved to Dubai in 2005, it took time to build confidence in expressing myself in a professional and social context. Public speaking, networking, and sharing ideas openly weren't easy at first. But art gave me the confidence to express myself in other ways. It taught me that expression isn't limited to words—it can be visual, emotional, and deeply personal.

As I continue to grow in my career and personal life, I now make a conscious effort to keep art in my routine. Whether it's sketching in the middle of a busy week, painting on a weekend, or simply observing colours and textures in everyday life, I know that creativity isn't just an escape—it's a necessity. Art, to me, is meditation in motion, a tool for clarity, and a lifelong companion in navigating the complexities of business and life.

Art has the ability to calm the mind, much like meditation. It allows us to be fully present, immersed in the process rather than the outcome. These exercises focus on using art as a meditative tool for relaxation and self-awareness.

EXERCISES

1. **Breath-Integrated Brushwork** – Synchronize your breathing with each brushstroke, inhaling deeply as you lift the brush and exhaling as you press it onto the canvas.
2. **Monochromatic Mandalas** – Create intricate mandalas using only one colour. The repetition and focus on symmetry encourage mindfulness.
3. **Nature Impression Sketching** – Spend time in nature and sketch organic shapes like leaves, waves, or trees, focusing only on the movement of your hand.

# THE ART OF LETTING GO

As I delved deeper into my artistic journey, I started to see how art and business were intertwined in ways I had never realized before. Art has this incredible ability to teach patience, resilience, and the art of letting go. When I first started sketching again after years of being caught up in my business, I found myself hesitating before making a stroke. The perfectionist in me, the same one that had helped me build a successful company, was also holding me back. I wanted every line to be perfect, every color to blend seamlessly, but art doesn't work that way—just like business doesn't.

I remember sitting with my sketchbook, staring at a blank page for what felt like hours. My mind was racing with thoughts of work, deadlines, clients, and the ever-present fear of making mistakes. But as I started drawing, something clicked. I realized that in art, as in business, you have to take risks. You have to put the first stroke down, even if you're not sure where it will lead. You have to trust the process.

Embracing Uncertainty

One of the biggest lessons art has taught me is how to embrace uncertainty. In business, there's a constant push for structure, planning, and control. We create strategies, forecasts, and risk assessments to minimize the unknown. But art doesn't operate within such rigid boundaries. It forces you to accept the unexpected

I recall a particular watercolor painting I was working on. I had envisioned a specific outcome, but as soon as the colors started bleeding into each other unpredictably, I felt a surge of frustration. My initial instinct was to try and "fix" it, to regain control. But then I stopped. Instead of fighting the flow, I let the water and pigment do what they wanted. The result? A piece that was far more beautiful than I had originally planned. It was a stark reminder that sometimes, letting go leads to the best outcomes—not just in art, but in business and life as well.

Mistakes as Opportunities

In my entrepreneurial journey, I have made my fair share of mistakes—trusting the wrong people, making poor investment choices, and at times, losing sight of the bigger picture. But just as in painting, where a wrong brushstroke can lead to an entirely new creative direction, mistakes in business often pave the way for innovation and growth.

I remember one of my earliest ventures, where a simple oversight in a business contract led to unexpected financial setbacks. At the time, it felt like the end of the world. But that mistake forced me to reassess my approach, to build better contracts, to trust my instincts more, and ultimately, to grow into a more resilient entrepreneur.

In art, you often hear the phrase, "happy accidents." Bob Ross popularized this idea, and I have come to embrace it fully. A misplaced stroke, an unintended color blend—these often lead to the most stunning results. This mind-set shift has helped me tremendously in my business as well. Instead of viewing failures as definitive roadblocks, I now see them as opportunities to learn and adapt.

The Art of Detachment

One of the most challenging aspects of both business and art is knowing when to step back. As an entrepreneur, I have always been deeply attached to my work. Every project, every pitch, every client interaction feels personal. But over time, I have learned that holding on too tightly can be counterproductive. Just as an artist must know when to stop refining a painting, a business leader must know when to step back and let things take their natural course.

This realization came to me during one of the most difficult periods of my career. My business was going through a downturn, and I was caught in an endless cycle of stress, overwork, and frustration. I tried to control every aspect, micromanage every detail, and in doing so, I was suffocating both myself and my team. It was only when I took a step back—both mentally and physically—that things started to improve.

Art played a huge role in this shift. Spending time sketching and painting allowed me to detach from the chaos of work. It reminded me that sometimes, the best thing you can do is take a breath, step back, and trust that you have laid a strong enough foundation for things to fall into place. The ability to detach, to trust the process, and to let things flow naturally is an invaluable lesson that art has taught me—and one that has made me a better leader.

Finding Freedom in Creation

Ultimately, the greatest lesson art has given me is the freedom to create without fear. In business, there is always an element of performance pressure. Targets, KPIs, investor expectations—all these factors can stifle creativity and lead to a fear of failure. But when I pick up a brush or a pencil, there are no expectations. There is no judgment. There is just me and the act of creation.

This freedom has slowly seeped into my approach to business as well. I no longer fear taking creative risks. I am more open to exploring unconventional ideas, to stepping outside my comfort zone, and to embracing innovation without the paralyzing fear of failure. Just as an artist must be willing to experiment with new techniques and styles, an entrepreneur must be willing to explore new strategies and approaches.

Art has taught me lessons that no business school ever could. It has shown me the beauty of imperfection, the power of resilience, and the importance of embracing the unknown. By integrating these lessons into my entrepreneurial journey, I have found greater balance, creativity, and fulfilment. The art of letting go is not just about creating beautiful paintings—it is about cultivating a mind-set that allows you to navigate both business and life with greater ease and confidence.

Letting go is a key aspect of creativity and personal growth. Art helps release control, embrace uncertainty, and accept imperfections.

EXERCISES

1. **Abstract Emotion Painting** – Use colours and strokes to express an emotion rather than a literal image, without worrying about how it looks.
2. **Destruction and Reconstruction Collage** – Create a piece, tear it apart, then use those pieces to build something new, symbolizing resilience and adaptation.
3. **Fluid Ink Play** – Use watercolours or ink, allowing them to flow naturally across the page without trying to control them.

ART AS A TOOL FOR IDEA GENERATION

Moving to Dubai in 2005 was a defining moment, not just professionally but personally. It was an entirely new environment—one that required adaptation at every level. Coming from India, where a common language formed the backbone of communication, Dubai's multicultural work culture was a stark contrast. The way businesses operated, how creativity was perceived, and how client relationships were managed—all of it was different. More than that, it was my first time truly being alone, away from my family, in a city where everything was unfamiliar

Adapting to this change wasn't easy. Communication skills that I had taken for granted suddenly felt inadequate. My confidence took a hit, and my naturally introverted nature only intensified the struggle. I had always preferred expressing myself through art rather than words, but now, I needed to reshape how I functioned. This period of transformation became an unexpected lesson in creativity. Just as in art, where an unfamiliar stroke or an unplanned texture can evolve into something meaningful, I had to embrace the discomfort of change and use it to generate new ideas.

Art became an outlet—a space where the pressure of adaptation wasn't daunting but freeing. Instead of worrying about how I would fit into this new culture, I channelled those emotions into creativity. In unfamiliar situations, the mind tends to retreat into known patterns, but through art, I discovered new perspectives. I saw that creativity wasn't just about the ability to draw, paint, or design; it was about problem-solving, about seeing connections where none seemed obvious before.

One of the biggest lessons came from understanding that creativity flourishes in discomfort. Just as an artist learns to work with constraints—limited colours, an uncooperative medium, or an unintended smudge—I had to work within the realities of my situation. The discomfort of speaking in a language that didn't feel natural, of managing clients with different expectations, and of navigating a new business landscape pushed me to think differently. Instead of resisting the unfamiliar, I started embracing it.

In the business world, people often talk about 'thinking outside the box.' But when you're placed in a completely new environment, it's not about stepping outside a box—it's about realising that the box itself can be redesigned. The techniques I used in art, whether it was experimenting with unexpected colour palettes or reworking a painting that didn't quite turn out as planned, became metaphors for how I approached my professional life.

Remodelling myself wasn't an overnight process. Just like in art, where layers build upon each other over time to create depth and meaning, I had to slowly piece together my confidence and adaptability. I became more observant—studying how people interacted, how they communicated their ideas, and how businesses operated.

Interestingly, the more I immersed myself in art, the better I became at generating ideas in business. Art forces you to see beyond the obvious—to find patterns in chaos, to connect dots that aren't immediately visible. This ability translated directly into how I tackled challenges at work. Where once I would have struggled to articulate my thoughts, I began finding ways to visually express them. I started using sketches and diagrams to explain concepts to clients and colleagues, turning my artistic instincts into a tool for communication.

The introversion that once held me back started to work in my favour. While I still wasn't the loudest voice in the room, I had found my way of contributing—through visual storytelling, through quiet but thoughtful leadership, and through an ability to approach problems with a creative lens. My experiences in Dubai taught me that idea generation isn't about waiting for inspiration to strike; it's about actively seeking new perspectives, about allowing yourself to be reshaped by the experiences around you.

Over time, the same principles I applied in art—curiosity, experimentation, and a willingness to embrace mistakes— became the foundation for my professional growth. I learned that discomfort isn't something to be avoided; it's something to be explored. Whether in art or in business, the most unexpected ideas often emerge from the most unfamiliar situations. And sometimes, the only way to truly innovate is to let go of preconceptions, pick up the brush, and start creating.

The Beauty of Imperfection

As a perfectionist, I struggled with the idea that mistakes were part of the process. In my early days of art, I would stress over every detail, trying to make each line and colour flawless. But art, like life, thrives on imperfection. Some of my best pieces happened when I made a 'mistake'—a misplaced stroke, an unexpected colour blend, an accidental texture. Rather than erasing them, I learned to incorporate them into the final piece, making them an essential part of the artwork's character.

This lesson has been invaluable in business. No strategy unfolds exactly as planned; no venture is free from unexpected turns. The most successful businesses pivot, adapt, and find beauty in the flaws. Learning to embrace imperfection has given me the confidence to take risks and trust the creative process in every aspect of my work.

Art as a Tool for Problem-Solving

Art has taught me lateral thinking—seeing problems from different angles, experimenting with unconventional solutions. When I get stuck in business, I turn to my sketchbook. It's amazing how stepping into an artistic mind-set opens up new ways of thinking. Sometimes, while sketching, an idea clicks in my mind that I hadn't considered before. The brain processes creativity differently when engaged in art, and that shift in perspective can be incredibly powerful in business.

One example that stands out is a time when my company faced a major restructuring challenge. Logical analysis wasn't providing clear answers, so I took a different approach. I started drawing mind maps and visual representations of the problem. It allowed me to see connections that weren't obvious before. This practice of visual thinking—using sketches, diagrams, and even abstract art—has become a valuable tool in my problem-solving approach.

Patience and Trusting the Process

Art teaches patience. A painting isn't completed in one sitting; it takes layers, refinement, and time. The same is true for business growth and personal development. In the fast-paced world of entrepreneurship, it's easy to get frustrated when things don't move as quickly as expected. But just like a painting evolves through careful attention and persistence, business success comes from steady effort over time.

I've had moments where I felt I wasn't progressing fast enough, both in art and in my career. But looking back, I realise that every step—even the slow, frustrating ones—was essential. The key is to trust the process, to keep working, and to embrace the journey rather than obsess over the end result.

Letting go is one of the hardest but most essential skills. Whether in art, business, or life, holding on too tightly to expectations can stifle growth. Art has given me the freedom to explore, to make mistakes, and to create without fear. That same mind-set has transformed how I approach challenges in my professional life. By embracing uncertainty, trusting creativity, and allowing ideas to flow naturally, I've found a sense of clarity that no rigid plan could have provided.

In the next chapter, we'll explore the role of art in leadership—how creativity fosters innovation, strengthens decision-making, and helps leaders navigate complexity with confidence.

Art helps break mental rigidity and encourages out-of-the-box thinking. It allows you to visualize abstract ideas in new ways.

EXERCISES

1. **Doodle Brainstorming** – While thinking about a challenge, freely doodle shapes, lines, or symbols. These random marks can lead to unexpected ideas.
2. **Random Object Sketching** – Take two unrelated objects and combine them into one drawing (e.g., a clock merged with a tree).
3. **Storyboarding Dreams** – Sketch key moments from a recent dream, allowing subconscious ideas to surface.

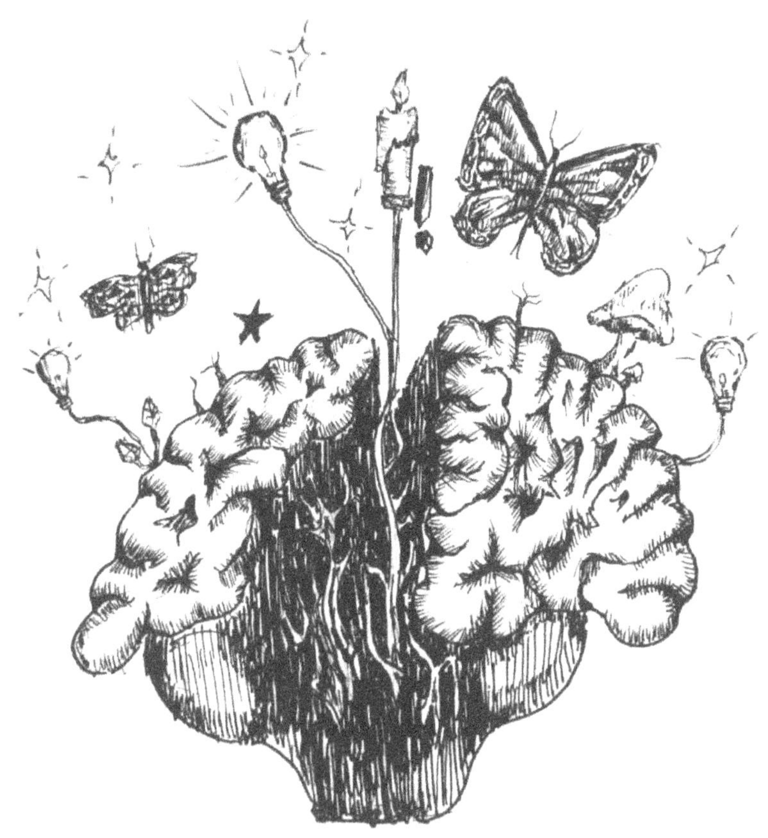

ART AS A MIND OPENER

Growing up, I always struggled with verbal expression. Coming from a Marathi vernacular medium school, English was not my first language, and for a long time, that held me back in social and professional settings. When I moved to Dubai in 2005, I realised how much of a barrier language could be. Not being able to articulate my thoughts confidently in English stopped me from sharing my ideas openly, and I often felt hesitant in conversations, especially in professional environments where clarity and persuasion were key. However, what I lacked in words, I found in art.

Art, for me, became a tool of communication beyond language. It allowed me to express emotions, thoughts, and perspectives without needing to find the right words. There was no pressure of grammar, pronunciation, or eloquence—just colours, lines, and textures that conveyed what I felt. Over time, I realised that art had given me something much greater than just a creative outlet; it had opened my mind to new ways of perceiving and understanding the world.

The Universality of Art

One of the most powerful aspects of art is its ability to transcend linguistic and cultural barriers. A painting, a sculpture, or even a simple sketch can be understood by people from completely different backgrounds. Art doesn't need translation. This realisation dawned on me when I started travelling more extensively. Whether I was in a small town in Italy admiring street art, or in a gallery in Japan observing traditional ink paintings, I could feel the emotions behind the work. I didn't need to understand the local language to connect with the essence of the piece.

This is something I have personally experienced in my work as well. In business, especially in a multicultural environment like the UAE, where people from different backgrounds come together, communication can sometimes be a challenge. I realised that using visual elements—whether in presentations, brainstorming sessions, or user experience designs—allowed me to convey ideas more effectively than words ever could. I started incorporating sketches into my business discussions, illustrating concepts instead of just explaining them verbally. It was surprising how much easier it became to align ideas when they were represented visually.

Art as an Enabler of Open-Mindedness

Art has the power to change perspectives. It forces you to see beyond the obvious, to look deeper, and to question assumptions. This is something that naturally happens when you create or even observe art. A single painting can be interpreted in multiple ways, and each observer might take away something different based on their personal experiences and emotions. This ability to see things from different perspectives is an essential trait of leadership and problem-solving.

Throughout my entrepreneurial journey, I've realised that the best leaders are those who remain open-minded. They are willing to see beyond the surface, to embrace multiple viewpoints, and to approach problems creatively. Art has trained me to do just that. When I look at a blank canvas, I no longer see just an empty space—I see possibilities. I see what could be, rather than what is. This mind-set has been incredibly valuable in business, where rigid thinking can often lead to missed opportunities.

There were moments in my career when I faced major setbacks—times when the business went through rough patches, when projects didn't go as planned, or when I felt creatively stuck. In those moments, I turned to art, not just as a distraction, but as a way to clear my mind. When I painted, I could detach from the immediate chaos and see things from a fresh perspective. It allowed me to approach problems differently, to see patterns and connections that weren't visible before.

Some of the biggest reasons for mental blocks and closed mind is the fear of change, fear of failure and fear of moving on from the comforts of where you are. But just like art is never created with any of these fears life can't be lived with those mental blocks and the best way to break those blocks is to take that first step, putting that first stroke or first drop of the paint, that first thought that can lead you to many more.

From Shyness to Public Speaking: The Power of Expression

Growing up, I was an introvert, not someone who enjoyed large social gatherings or speaking up in public. Expressing my thoughts verbally was never my strength, and I often found myself feeling disconnected from conversations. But where words failed me, art stepped in as a bridge. It became my way of expressing emotions, ideas, and perspectives that I struggled to articulate.

Even when I ventured into business, my reserved nature persisted. In a world that often rewards those who can confidently articulate their ideas, I found myself relying on the visual language of art. I used sketches and diagrams to convey complex ideas in meetings, and over time, I realized that this ability to communicate visually set me apart. It became a tool to break down barriers, engage stakeholders, and inspire teams. This realisation also played a crucial role in helping me develop confidence in public speaking. Today, when I stand on stage at conferences and panels, speaking about design, business, and user experience, I credit my ability to express ideas to the years of practice I unknowingly had through art.

For an introvert like me, social interactions have never been easy. While I have gradually become more comfortable speaking in public, thanks to years of experience, there was a time when it was one of my biggest fears. I would often hesitate to express my opinions in group discussions, feeling that my words might not come out right. But with art, there was no hesitation.

I remember a specific instance from my early career when I had to present an idea to a group of senior executives. Instead of explaining my concept in a traditional way, I sketched it out on a whiteboard. To my surprise, not only did they understand my vision immediately, but they also engaged in a more interactive discussion around it. That was when I truly realised the power of visual communication. It was a turning point for me, and since then, I have consciously integrated art into how I communicate complex ideas.

Even outside of work, art has helped me connect with people in ways that words never could. During my travels, I often carry a sketchbook with me. I sketch scenes, people, and places, and sometimes, strangers come up to me, intrigued by what I'm drawing. It sparks conversations—conversations that go beyond language, beyond cultural differences. Some of my most memorable interactions have happened simply because of a sketch I was working on.

Embracing the Imperfections

One of the greatest lessons art has taught me is the power of imperfection. When you start working on a painting, you have an idea—a vision of what you want to create. But as the colours mix, as unexpected strokes appear, as the medium behaves in unpredictable ways, the final outcome is rarely what you initially imagined. And that is where the beauty lies—in adaptation, in responding to the unexpected rather than resisting it.

Mistakes in a painting do not necessarily ruin it; sometimes, they add character. The same applies to business—what appears to be a misstep can often lead to something new, something unexpected, something even better than the original plan.

Creative blocks happen to everyone. In art, I've had moments where inspiration felt out of reach, where every idea seemed dull. In business, there were times when strategies failed, markets shifted overnight, or setbacks made progress seem impossible. The common factor in both is resistance—the inner force that keeps us stuck.

One of the biggest lessons I've taken from art is the value of stepping away. I used to believe that persistence alone would break a block, but sometimes, the best thing to do is pause. Just like walking away from a painting and returning with fresh eyes, taking breaks in business has often brought clarity. When I revisit a problem with a clear mind, the solution presents itself naturally.

Mental blocks are often the biggest barriers to growth. The fear of making mistakes can be paralysing, stopping us from trying. In art, the blank canvas brings hesitation—the second-guessing, the worry that it won't be perfect. But the only way forward is to start.

The Long Game

Art has taught me endurance—a quality essential for creativity and overcoming mental blocks. A painting is not completed in an instant. Each layer, each stroke, requires time to dry, to settle, to interact with what came before and what will come next. Rushing the process often leads to chaos, smudging what could have been a masterpiece.

Creative blocks can feel like an impassable wall, but art has shown me that patience and persistence are the keys to breaking through. Just as a painting unfolds gradually, inspiration and clarity arrive in their own time. The more I tried to force an idea, the more elusive it became. But stepping back, allowing thoughts to breathe, and trusting the process often led to breakthroughs.

The long game in art—and in thought—is about keeping the larger vision in mind. It's easy to get caught up in small missteps, a stroke that feels off, an idea that doesn't immediately take shape. But a painting is never about a single brushstroke, just as a concept isn't about one fleeting thought. The bigger picture is what matters. The key is to keep moving forward, to allow the process to unfold, knowing that mistakes are just part of the journey. A wrong stroke does not ruin the canvas—it becomes part of the final composition, sometimes in ways you never expected.

Early in my journey, I often found myself frustrated when ideas wouldn't flow as quickly as I wanted. But through art, I learned that everything has its own rhythm. Some concepts need time to mature, some visions need space to evolve. The mind, like a canvas, benefits from layers of thought, from moments of stillness as much as movement. The best creative insights often come when you stop resisting and start embracing the ebb and flow of the process. The long game is about trusting that, in time, everything will come together.

The Art of Moving Forward

Every stroke in a painting, even the ones that seem misplaced at first, contributes to the final composition. What may seem like an error in the moment often becomes an integral part of the artwork, adding depth and character. Art has taught me that mistakes are not the end—they are just part of the journey.

Creativity requires embracing uncertainty, being open to change, and learning to find beauty in the unexpected. The more I reflect on my experiences, the more I see how art has trained my mind to break through limitations. Mental blocks often stem from fear—fear of making the wrong move, fear of imperfection, fear of not meeting expectations. But just as a blank canvas can be intimidating, the only way to overcome the hesitation is to start.

The most important lesson? The process itself is just as valuable as the outcome. Art has shown me that progress isn't always linear. Some ideas take time to evolve, some concepts need to be revisited, and sometimes, the best breakthroughs come from accidents. The key is to keep moving forward, to trust in exploration, and to allow creativity to unfold without rigid expectations.

Engaging in different perspectives through art expands our thinking. It allows us to see beyond our usual ways of interpreting the world.

EXERCISES

1. **Perspective Flip Drawing** – Draw an everyday object from an unusual angle (e.g., an extreme close-up or an upside-down view).
2. **Cultural Art Exploration** – Recreate an art style from a culture different from your own to challenge familiarity and expand visual vocabulary.
3. **Sensory Drawing** – Create art based on senses other than sight, like drawing the texture of sound or the feeling of warmth.

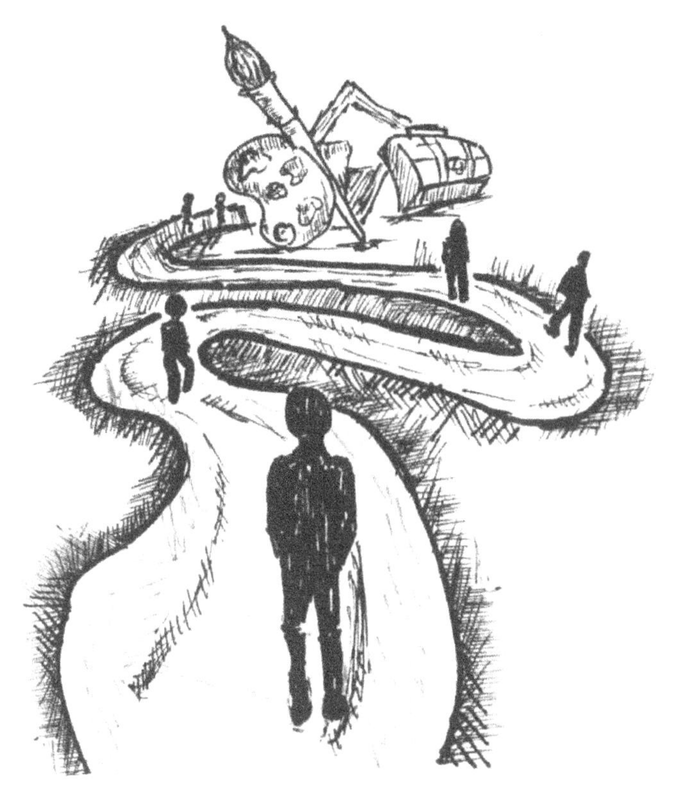

ART AND LEADERSHIP

Art has a unique way of teaching patience, a trait often overlooked in leadership but essential for long-term success. Whether it's refining a painting or leading a team through challenges, both require a level of resilience that comes only through experience. For me, patience was never my strong suit. I always wanted results immediately, whether in business or personal projects. However, art had a way of forcing me to slow down, observe, and accept that mistakes were just part of the process.

In school, I was the one who would help others with their drawings, carefully sketching science diagrams and intricate Rangoli patterns. Back then, I didn't fully understand that this skill wasn't just about technical ability—it was about seeing details others missed, being persistent, and refining things until they felt just right. Years later, as I ventured into business, I realised that these same principles applied to leadership.

The Frame of Leadership

Leadership and creativity are often seen as two distinct domains—one structured, goal-driven, and pragmatic, while the other is expressive, boundless, and deeply personal. Yet, as these thoughts have unfolded, the parallels between them become undeniable. The journey through art and leadership has never been about following a formula or reaching a defined destination. It has been about embracing imperfections, learning through mistakes, and finding ways to express and adapt in ever-changing circumstances.

There is a common misconception that leadership is defined by loud voices, aggressive decisions, and an unyielding presence. But just as art doesn't always need to be bold, provocative, or loud to make an impact, leadership also takes many forms. Some of the most effective leaders lead with quiet confidence, by listening more than they speak, by observing before acting, and by fostering an environment where creativity and different perspectives thrive. Similarly, art can be soothing, subtle, and introspective, yet still immensely powerful. Whether on a canvas or within a team, both require calmness, an eye for balance, and an appreciation for evolution over time.

Teaching Leadership Through Example

One of the biggest lessons art has taught me is that leadership isn't about telling people what to do—it's about showing them how to navigate uncertainty. When I sketch, I don't always have a clear plan. Sometimes, I let the lines and shapes evolve organically, trusting the process. In business, I apply the same philosophy: I encourage my team to experiment, to take risks, and to see mistakes as opportunities to refine and grow.

I've had team members come to me, frustrated over a project that didn't go as expected. Instead of offering an immediate solution, I encourage them to step back, analyse, and find a way to turn things around—just like I do with an unfinished painting. This ability to pause, reassess, and move forward with a fresh perspective is something I owe entirely to my artistic background.

Learning Through Mistakes

One of the most frustrating aspects of art is making a mistake— especially when you're deep into a piece and suddenly realise that one wrong stroke has changed everything. In my early days, I used to abandon paintings if I felt they weren't going the way I envisioned. But over time, I learned that fixing mistakes, layering over them, correcting them, or even incorporating them into the final piece often led to unexpectedly beautiful results.

Leadership, I found, worked the same way. I didn't wake up one day with all the answers. I made wrong decisions, trusted the wrong people, and, at times, questioned whether I was even cut out for this journey. But just like in art, leadership is about persistence—seeing the bigger picture and understanding that mistakes don't define the final outcome. They are simply part of the process.

From Perfection to Growth

When I started my business, I had a very rigid idea of success. I believed that if I made the right decisions and worked hard, things would fall into place. But business, like art, is never a straight line. There are setbacks, challenges, and moments of self-doubt. What I learned through both art and leadership is that focusing too much on perfection is often counterproductive.

There was a phase when I became obsessed with getting every detail right in a painting. I would erase and redo lines multiple times, only to realise that overworking it drained the energy out of the piece. Similarly, in leadership, I have seen how micromanaging or obsessing over small imperfections can demotivate a team and slow down progress. Letting go of the need for perfection and embracing adaptability became a crucial turning point in both my art and business journey.

I was a rigid leader. I had my ways, my opinions, often driven by my hunger for perfection. Then as I started looking at my art differently, my approach towards leadership changed too. Much like how I approach art, I have learned to adapt, to take failures and mistakes as part of the process rather than as signs of incompetence. The ability to change direction without losing sight of the bigger picture is an art in itself, and it is something that both leaders and artists must master.

The same applies to leadership. Many hesitate to take risks, fearing the wrong decision. But just as an artist must trust the process, a leader must trust their ability to navigate challenges. No decision is perfect, but inaction is always worse than movement.

Resilience: The Common Thread Between Art and Leadership

I've had tough moments in business—moments where I questioned everything. During one particularly difficult time, when my business faced a major setback, I turned to painting as a way to cope. I was working on a large canvas, layering colours, making mistakes, and trying to correct them. At some point, I realised that what I was doing on the canvas was exactly what I needed to do in my business—step back, take a breath, and trust the process.

Resilience in leadership isn't just about pushing forward no matter what. It's about learning when to pause, when to adjust, and when to completely rethink your approach. Art has taught me that sometimes, walking away for a moment and coming back with a fresh perspective is the best thing you can do.

In business and leadership, the ability to see beyond the immediate problem is crucial. Just as an artist sees potential in a blank canvas, a leader must see potential in challenges, in people, and in opportunities that others might overlook. The best solutions are often not the most obvious ones, and creativity is what allows us to find those hidden solutions.

The Balance Between Control and Freedom

One of the most fascinating aspects of art is the balance between control and freedom. While there is a degree of technique and precision required, the most beautiful works often emerge when the artist lets go of total control and allows the medium to guide them.

Leadership, too, requires this balance. A leader must set direction, provide structure, and make critical decisions, but they must also give their teams the freedom to explore, innovate, and bring their own strengths to the table.

Micromanagement stifles creativity. If an artist focuses too much on controlling every detail, the artwork loses its spontaneity and depth. Similarly, if a leader tries to control every aspect of their team's work, they stifle creativity and innovation. True leadership, like true artistry, lies in knowing when to guide and when to step back.

Trusting the people, you lead, just as an artist trusts their brush to move with instinct rather than rigidity, creates an environment where ideas flourish. Some of the most powerful breakthroughs—whether in art or business—come when control is balanced with the freedom to explore, take risks, and even fail.

At its core, both art and leadership are about vision. They require the ability to see beyond the present moment, to imagine what could be, and to bring that vision to life. They demand patience, resilience, and the willingness to embrace the unknown. And most importantly, they remind us that while we may never have full control over the outcome, the process itself holds immense value.

Leadership is not just about decision-making; it's about vision, patience, and adaptability—qualities that can be honed through art.

EXERCISES

1. **Vision Board Creation** – Make a collage of images, textures, and colours that represent your leadership style and aspirations.
2. **Team Mural Project** – Collaborate with others to create a shared artwork, learning to balance different perspectives.
3. **Reflective Self-Portrait** – Paint a self-portrait that symbolically represents your leadership journey.

THE PARALLEL PATHS OF ART AND BUSINESS

Looking back, I can see how much of my approach to business was shaped by my natural inclination toward art and, at the same time, by my introverted nature. I never thought of myself as a conventional entrepreneur—someone who walks into a room and owns the conversation. In fact, I was quite the opposite. Social interactions, large gatherings, and networking events always felt like a challenge. But while I struggled with verbal expression, I always found in visual storytelling. Art had already been my voice long before business came into the picture, and it continues to shape how I think, strategies, and communicate in ways that words alone never could.

It took me a while to understand that the way I navigate business is deeply rooted in the same principles that define art. Just as a blank canvas invites creativity, problem-solving in business requires vision and imagination. A single brushstroke in the wrong place doesn't mean failure—it means adaptation, learning, and resilience. Similarly, a business decision that doesn't go as planned isn't the end; it's an opportunity to adjust, refine, and approach the challenge with a new perspective.

Business as a Creative Process

When I started my business, I didn't do it with a clear, grand plan or end goal in mind. Much like my journey in art, it was something I embraced along the way. There was no strategic roadmap that led me here—just the willingness to take on what came my way, to experiment, to learn from mistakes, and to evolve as things unfolded. I never set out to build a company with a vision of becoming a dominant player in a specific field. I just wanted to do meaningful work, solve problems creatively, and bring something different to the table. In hindsight, my business decisions were never purely transactional or analytical. They were intuitive, guided by a perspective honed by years of creative thinking.

One of the most significant ways in which art and business have overlapped in my life is in their ability to embrace change. When you work on a painting, you rarely end up exactly where you expected to when you first started. What begins as a rough idea takes shape organically, influenced by instinct, mistakes, and unexpected inspirations along the way. Business works the same way. No amount of planning can predict every twist and turn. The key is to stay open to iteration, to pivot when needed, and to embrace imperfection as part of the process.

The Role of Constraints in Driving Innovation

Another parallel I've noticed is the role of constraints. In art, you're often limited by materials, time, or space. A certain brush might not give you the effect you envisioned, a colour might mix differently than expected, or the paper might react in an unpredictable way. But within those constraints, creativity thrives. The same applies to business. Limited resources, market challenges, and unexpected setbacks force you to think differently, to innovate, and to work within your limitations to create something unique. If everything were predictable, neither art nor business would be half as interesting.

When resources are constrained, true ingenuity emerges. Many of the most ground-breaking business models and innovations come not from excess but from necessity. Whether it's working within tight budgets, finding unconventional solutions, or adapting to an ever-changing landscape, the ability to create under constraints is what separates those who struggle from those who thrive. Some of the most valuable lessons I've learned in business have come from moments where things didn't go according to plan—where I had to rethink, reframe, and rebuild. Those moments weren't failures; they were necessary disruptions that forced me to think differently.

Patterns, Intuition, and Originality

When I reflect on my business journey, I realise that a lot of what I did was simply applying artistic thinking to business problems. Where others saw rigid processes, I saw compositions that could be reworked. Where others looked at metrics, I looked at patterns. And where others sought competition, I sought originality. This is why I have never fully separated my creative side from my entrepreneurial side—they are simply two expressions of the same mind-set.

At the heart of both art and business is the ability to see the world differently. To question norms, to explore new possibilities, and to find meaning in the abstract. Art teaches you to observe beyond the obvious, to interpret what's not immediately visible, and to find structure within chaos. Business, when approached with the same mind-set, becomes more than just numbers and strategies—it becomes a canvas for innovation, for storytelling, and for crafting something truly impactful.

The Freedom to Define Your Own Path

If there's one thing I've learned from balancing both worlds, it's that there is no single right way to do things. Some artists meticulously plan every detail of their work before making a mark, while others let intuition guide them, allowing the piece to evolve naturally. Business follows the same spectrum. Some people thrive on structured plans, while others, like me, find comfort in adaptability. What matters is understanding your own way of working and staying true to it, even when the world expects you to conform.

I never set out to draw parallels between my love for art and my journey in business—it just happened. Over time, I began to realise that the same creative energy that drove me to sketch, paint, and experiment on canvas was also shaping my decisions as an entrepreneur. I used to think that art and business were two separate worlds, but now I know they are deeply intertwined. Whether I'm holding a paintbrush or running a project, the principles remain the same: observe deeply, embrace mistakes, trust intuition, and keep creating.

Creativity and business are deeply connected. Art teaches problem-solving, resourcefulness, and adaptation—critical skills in business.

EXERCISES

1. **Product Lifecycle Illustration** – Draw or paint a visual representation of how an idea or product evolves over time.
2. **Business Concept Sketching** – Turn a business challenge into a visual diagram or metaphorical artwork.
3. **Market Dynamics Collage** – Create a collage of images that represent shifts in the industry, allowing intuitive analysis of patterns.

INCORPORATING ART INTO DAILY LIFE

Art has never been just an activity or a profession for me—it has been an integral part of my existence, shaping how I perceive the world, communicate my thoughts, and even conduct business. While I have never pursued art with the intent of becoming a great artist, it has quietly guided me through the different phases of my life, even when I wasn't fully aware of its impact. Looking back, I see how art seeped into every aspect of my life, influencing my mind-set, my leadership approach, and even my ability to express myself in ways that words often failed to convey.

The Art of Minimalism

Minimalism in art is not just about reduction—it is about essence. It is about stripping away the excess to reveal what truly matters. A single stroke on a blank canvas can carry more weight than a flurry of colours, just as a single word can sometimes say more than a paragraph. I have found this to be true not only in my artistic practice but in life itself.

Minimalism is an aesthetic choice, but it is also a philosophy. It teaches restraint and the power of simplicity. Whether it is the minimalism of strokes, of shapes, of forms, or of composition, each element is intentional. This is something that has also influenced the way I live—what I wear, what I eat, and even how I structure my days. There is beauty in repetition, in consistency, in knowing that less is often more.

Just as an artist carefully selects each line and colour to create a meaningful composition, we must curate our thoughts with intention. Knowing which ideas to hold onto, which ones to let go, which ones to act upon, and which ones to nurture is an art in itself. This form of minimalism is not about suppressing thoughts but about filtering them for efficiency, for clarity, and for peace of mind.

An endless loop of 'what ifs' and scenarios that never materialise. But minimalism in thinking allows space for focus and purpose. It is about removing mental clutter so that the thoughts that truly matter can flourish. It creates a sense of calm, a mental discipline that enables creativity, decision-making, and emotional balance.

Much like in art, where negative space is as important as the elements within a painting, the space between thoughts is equally significant. In that space lies clarity, understanding, and the ability to move forward with a mind that is light, unburdened, and free.

But minimalism does not mean deprivation. It is not about denying oneself the finer things in life, but rather about experiencing them with intention. It is not about how many possessions one has or how frequently one indulges, but about the depth of appreciation for each experience. Minimalism in thought is perhaps the most profound of all—learning to declutter the mind, to focus on what truly matters, and to find clarity amidst the noise.

Art has taught me that minimalism is not just a style but a way of being. It is the ability to see the essence of things, to appreciate the space between, and to understand that sometimes, what is left unsaid is just as powerful as what is spoken.

Blurring the Lines Between Art and Work

One of the biggest misconceptions people have is that art and work are two separate entities. But for me, the boundaries between them have always been blurred. Whether it was in strategy meetings, brainstorming sessions, or presentations, I found myself instinctively incorporating elements of art. From sketching user flows to visualizing abstract ideas, art became an essential part of my problem-solving toolkit.

In the digital space, where I have spent most of my career, the importance of visual thinking cannot be overstated. Good design is not just about aesthetics; it is about communication, engagement, and experience. The same principles that guide an artist—composition, balance, contrast—are the ones that guide a good user experience. My background in art has helped me navigate these principles effortlessly, giving me an edge in understanding the nuances of user behaviour and design thinking.

Bringing Art into Everyday Life

Art is often seen as something separate from daily life, something that requires dedicated time or special skills. But I have come to see it differently. Art does not have to be confined to a studio or a canvas. It can be integrated into the smallest aspects of life—how you arrange your workspace, how you choose your clothes, how you cook a meal, how you document your travels.

For me, one of the simplest ways I incorporate art into my daily life is by carrying a sketchbook wherever I go. Whenever I travel, instead of just taking photos, I sketch. Instead of writing long notes, I draw diagrams. These small acts keep my creative side engaged and help me see the world through a different lens.

I have also found that surrounding myself with art—whether it is my own or that of others—has a profound impact on my mind-set. My workspace is filled with sketches, paintings, and visual inspirations that serve as constant reminders of creativity and perspective. Even in the most stressful moments, a glance at a piece of art can shift my mind-set and bring a sense of calm.

The Unfinished Masterpiece

If there is one thing that art has taught me, it is that nothing is ever truly finished. A painting, a sketch, a business, a personal journey—everything is a work in progress. There is always room to refine, to evolve, to experiment. This perspective has been invaluable, not just in my creative pursuits but in my professional and personal life as well.

Too often, we get caught up in the pursuit of perfection, fearing failure or judgment. But art has shown me that imperfection is where growth happens. The best pieces are often the ones that carry unexpected textures, the ones that tell a story of struggle and correction. And life is no different. We are all creating our own masterpiece—one stroke at a time.

Mistakes have been the greatest teacher—both In creating and in leading. A misplaced stroke on a painting doesn't always mean failure; sometimes, it leads to unexpected beauty. The same applies to decision-making in business and leadership. Some of the hardest lessons have come from trusting the wrong people, making flawed choices, or navigating through periods of uncertainty. But these moments have shaped perspectives, refined instincts, and ultimately contributed to a deeper understanding of what it means to create and lead with authenticity.

The journey into self-expression has also been a lesson in communication. Coming from a background where language was once a barrier, art provided an avenue to communicate thoughts and emotions without words. Over time, this has translated into business and leadership, where storytelling, visual thinking, and non-verbal cues have played an essential role in influencing and guiding teams. Leadership isn't about controlling every aspect—it's about creating a space where ideas flow, where trust exists, and where growth happens organically.

Beyond the professional aspects, creativity has been a grounding force. As responsibilities increased and the complexities of running a business grew, art became a way to step back, reflect, and find clarity. It provided a form of meditation, a way to disconnect from the immediate chaos and reconnect with a deeper sense of purpose. The ability to shift between the structured world of leadership and the fluid world of art has brought balance, reminding that even in the most structured environments, creativity is an essential force.

Ultimately, the connection between creativity and leadership isn't something that was strategically planned or deliberately pursued. It emerged through experience, through trial and error, through moments of both doubt and discovery. There has never been an attempt to master either completely, but rather to embrace them both as continuous learning processes. Whether in art, in business, or in leadership, the journey is never about achieving perfection—it is about embracing imperfections, evolving with time, and finding expression in every step of the way.

Making art a part of daily routine enhances mindfulness, self-expression, and even productivity.

EXERCISES

1. **Daily Sketch Journal** – Sketch something from your day, no matter how simple, to build a habit of creative observation.
2. **Creative Cooking Plating** – Arrange food artistically before eating, transforming an everyday task into a creative ritual.
3. **Decorative Note-Taking** – Add small doodles or creative lettering to your to-do lists or notes.

ART AND THE CANVAS OF LIFE

It has dawned upon me that art has always been more than just a medium of expression for me. It has been a way of life, a philosophy, a silent teacher that has guided me through pernal triumphs and tribulations without me realising it till I sat down to think about it. Much like an artist layering paint onto a canvas, life layers' experiences onto us—sometimes in expected, deliberate strokes, and other times in chaotic, unpredictable splashes. My relationship with art has not only shaped my professional journey but has profoundly influenced my personal life, especially my experiences with relationships, parenthood, and personal resilience.

Art has also shaped the way I perceive relationships. I must admit that I haven't always been successful in them. While some people in life have been fleeting, others have left lasting imprints, much like the layers of paint on a canvas—some visible, others buried beneath the surface, yet still integral to the final composition. The lessons I have learned from art— the acceptance of imperfection—have echoed in my personal relationships, teaching me that not everything needs to be controlled or defined. Sometimes, the most beautiful things emerge when you allow space for spontaneity, for growth, for unexpected strokes to alter the composition.

However, there are relationships that stand out as deeply significant, none more so than the one I share with my daughter. The act of creation requires time, observation, and an openness to change—qualities that are equally essential in raising a child. I have often found myself applying the same principles of artistic growth to my parenting journey. Just as a painting goes through multiple stages, requiring revisions and refinements, so too does parenthood demand adaptability and an understanding that no two paths are the same.

One of the most beautiful moments I have shared with my daughter is co-creating art with her. Though these moments have not been as frequent as I would have liked, they remain some of the most cherished. In the beginning, I found myself unconsciously trying to impose my artistic style onto her, expecting her visual expression to mirror mine. But I quickly realized that her artistic voice was her own, unique and uninhibited, and that my role was not to shape it but to encourage it. I had to learn to step back, to allow her creativity to breathe without imposing my own artistic biases. That shift in mind-set wasn't just about art; it was a lesson in parenting and relationship. It taught me to embrace her individuality, to nurture her self-discovery rather than shaping her into something predefined.

Over time, I also realised that creativity for her did not necessarily reside in visual art. While she engaged in drawing and painting as a child, her true form of creative expression evolved into something else. Story writing, song writing, melody, lyrics—this became her medium of storytelling and self-reflection. And once again, I found myself in a position of learning. I understood that art, in any form, is a language of the soul. It isn't confined to a brush or a canvas. It could be words, notes, movement—anything that allows a person to express their innermost world. Watching her find her artistic voice in other forms reminded me that creativity, much like life, is fluid. It isn't meant to be contained within predefined structures.

This reaffirmed something I have always believed: art is not confined to a canvas; it exists in every form of self-expression. Whether through painting, music, writing, or any other medium, creativity is a dialogue between the inner self and the outer world, and every individual has their own language in which to speak it.

I was raised in a household where discipline, restraint and structure coexisted with creativity. My parents, both teachers, instilled in me a strong sense of perseverance, discipline, and resilience. However, their grounding principles were not rigid; they allowed me to explore my passion for design and art, even after my father passed away just after my second year of design school. My mother's unwavering support ensured that I could continue my education and follow my chosen path. Her belief in me was a guiding force. Many people tend to replicate the parenting styles they were raised with, often without question. I, too, had that inclination, but art had taught me something different. It had instilled in me the ability to observe, to reflect, and most importantly, to embrace change. Just as an artist adapts to a changing canvas, I learned to adapt my parenting approach. I recognised that my daughter was growing up in a world vastly different from the one I grew up in. The lessons of my childhood were valuable, but they could not be applied rigidly. I had to evolve, to rethink my approach, and to create a parenting style that was responsive rather than reactive. I have learned to observe her, understand her evolving worldview, and create a space where she can flourish on her own terms.

Seeing her grow, witnessing her triumphs, and even her struggles, fills me with a deep sense of pride. Each moment with her—whether in conversation, in silence, in laughter, or in the act of creating—becomes a brushstroke in the larger painting of our bond. And just as in art, I have learned to embrace every shade, every stroke, and every unfinished edge, knowing that it is all part of something far more beautiful than I could ever have planned.

Art has also been a pillar of support during some of the most difficult moments of my life. When my mother faced health crisis and, later, in the wake of her passing, art became my refuge. It helped me navigate the paradox of detachment and deep emotional connection. While I had to learn to let go, I also had to channel my empathy—not cantering my own grief but focusing on her journey, her suffering, and her peace. Losing a parent is a moment that shifts everything, and yet, through that pain, I found solace in creation. I realised that detachment doesn't mean a lack of love—it means understanding that love exists beyond the tangible, beyond the physical presence of someone.

If there is one thing that art has reinforced in my personal life, it is that creation and experience are inseparable. Art does not exist in isolation from the artist's journey. Similarly, life cannot be separated from the lessons it imparts. The patience to refine a painting, the courage to start over when something doesn't feel right, the wisdom to know when a piece is complete—all of these are life lessons, disguised as artistic techniques.

Ultimately, this chapter of my life—both as an artist and as a father—is about learning to let go while still holding on. Art has given me the ability to appreciate transience, to cherish what is in front of me without being consumed by the fear of loss. My daughter is my greatest source of inspiration, and just as a painting evolves with every brushstroke, our relationship continues to grow, shaped by the lessons that art has imparted to me.

Art mirrors life, capturing emotions, transitions, and personal narratives in visual form.

EXERCISES

1. **Life Timeline Mural** – Create a large-scale timeline of key life moments, using imagery and colour to represent emotions.
2. **Goal Visualization Painting** – Paint a symbolic representation of where you see yourself in the future.
3. **Emotion Wheel Artwork** – Create a circular chart where each section represents a different emotion you've experienced recently.

FINDING HAPPINESS THROUGH ART

Art has always been a mirror of human emotion—a reflection of our joys, sorrows, aspirations, and fears. But beyond being a medium of expression, art is a source of happiness, a bridge to deeper fulfilment that many of us overlook. We often associate happiness with achievements, possessions, or milestones, but art reminds us that joy can be found in the simplest of acts: a brushstroke, a melody, a sculpted form taking shape under our hands.

When you stand in front of an abstract painting, what you see isn't just shapes, colours, and textures—it's a reflection of your own state of mind. The same piece of art can evoke peace in one person and unease in another. Someone struggling with inner turmoil might see chaos in a seemingly random arrangement of brushstrokes, while another person in a more positive emotional space might perceive harmony in the very same strokes. This is what makes abstract art so powerful: it does not dictate meaning; it invites dialogue between the artwork and the observer.

This reflective quality of art goes beyond just visual perception. It taps into the subconscious, bringing to the surface emotions that might not be immediately obvious. Sometimes, a piece of art resonates with us for reasons we can't quite explain—we just feel something when we look at it. That "something" is often a reflection of our internal world.

This is why people have vastly different reactions to the same artwork. Two individuals standing side by side, looking at the same abstract painting, will see different things because they are bringing their own experiences, thoughts, and emotions into the interpretation. In this way, art doesn't just express—it listens. It becomes a silent conversation, a non-verbal dialogue between the self and something external.

For the artist, this phenomenon is equally intriguing. Once a piece is created and released into the world, it no longer belongs solely to its creator. It becomes something fluid, changing based on who interacts with it. What the artist originally felt while creating it might not be what the viewer perceives at all. And that's the beauty of it—art, especially abstract art, doesn't impose a single truth. It offers a space where every person can find their own meaning, their own reflection, their own story.

This is why art, at its core, is not just about aesthetics or technique. It is about connection—connection to oneself, to emotions, and to the countless interpretations that make every piece alive in a different way for each person.

I've spent years navigating both the business and creative worlds, and I've come to realise that the happiness derived from art isn't about talent or mastery. It's about engagement. It's about losing yourself in creation, in observing, in allowing something intangible to take form. This connection between art and happiness isn't just anecdotal—it's deeply rooted in how our brains respond to creativity.

The Science of Art and Joy

Studies have shown that engaging with art—whether creating or simply observing—triggers the release of dopamine, the neurotransmitter linked to pleasure and reward. This explains why we feel a rush of excitement when we complete a painting, why a beautifully composed photograph can uplift our mood, or why walking through an art gallery can be as stimulating as listening to our favourite song.

In fact, neuroscientists like Semir Zeki have found that simply looking at artwork we find beautiful activates the brain's frontal cortex, creating feelings of pleasure similar to those experienced when falling in love. Art engages us emotionally in ways that other experiences don't—it doesn't just show us something; it makes us *feel*.

But the happiness derived from art goes beyond mere observation. It's in the act of creating. There's something inherently joyful about working with our hands, experimenting with colours, shaping raw materials into something meaningful. This aligns with the idea of *effort-driven reward*, where physical engagement—whether painting, sculpting, or even crafting—stimulates a deeper sense of satisfaction and well-being.

Creativity and the Pursuit of Happiness

One of the most compelling aspects of art is how it taps into our innate desire to create. We often think of creativity as a skill reserved for artists, but in reality, it's an essential part of being human. From the cave paintings of our ancestors to the digital art of today, creativity has always been tied to our sense of purpose and joy.

Why? Because the act of creating allows us to explore, to discover, and to bring something new into existence. It gives us control over a small part of the world, a space where we set the rules. There's a sense of liberation in this—a break from the structured, logical thinking that dominates our daily lives.

I've seen this first-hand. In conversations with entrepreneurs, designers, and professionals from various fields, a common theme emerges: the moments they feel most fulfilled aren't necessarily tied to success in the traditional sense. Instead, it's when they're engaged in creating something—whether a product, a concept, or a piece of art.

Happiness, in many ways, is tied to *the process*. It's not about the final outcome, but the journey of making, experimenting, and seeing ideas come to life.

Art as a Tool for Connection

Beyond personal happiness, art also plays a crucial role in how we connect with others. Think about the shared experience of watching a film, the way music unites people at concerts, or how a single painting can evoke different emotions in different viewers. Art is one of the most powerful tools for communication—it allows us to express what words sometimes cannot.

I've always been fascinated by how art creates emotional resonance. A simple sketch can hold memories. A photograph can freeze time. A song can transport us to another moment in our lives. This connection between art and memory is another reason why it contributes to happiness—it anchors us to meaningful experiences, making us more present, more aware of the beauty around us.

In a world where we are often consumed by productivity and efficiency, art invites us to pause. It reminds us to *feel*. It creates spaces where we can share, understand, and relate to each other in ways that go beyond the surface.

The Everyday Joy of Art

One of the biggest misconceptions about art is that it belongs in galleries, that it's meant for the trained, the skilled, the professionals. But some of the purest joy comes from engaging with art in its simplest forms.

It's the quick sketch on a napkin. The doodles in the margins of a notebook. The spontaneous dance in the living room. The random snapshots taken on a walk. Art isn't just about masterpieces—it's about moments.

And in those moments, happiness is found. Not in perfection, not in accolades, but in the act of doing, of creating, of letting go of expectation and simply enjoying the process.

When we embrace art as part of our daily lives—not as a separate discipline, but as a natural extension of who we are—we begin to see its true power. We realise that happiness doesn't have to be something we chase. Sometimes, it's found in the stroke of a brush, the blending of colours, the rhythm of a song, or the lines of a sketch.

Art is an invitation to joy. The only question is: are we willing to accept it?

Art fosters joy by engaging our senses and allowing us to create something that resonates with our emotions.

EXERCISES

1. **Joy Collage** – Collect and arrange images, textures, and colours that make you feel happy.
2. **Happy Memory Illustration** – Sketch or paint a scene that brings back positive emotions.
3. **Intuitive Colour Play** – Without planning, choose colours that make you feel good and paint abstract shapes freely.

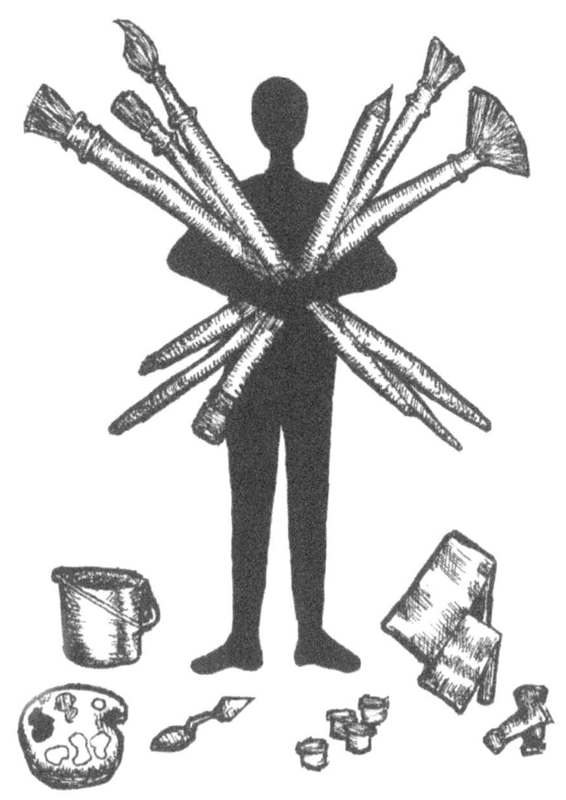

YOU ARE NEVER LONELY WITH ART

oneliness is a profound and pervasive emotion that touches individuals across all walks of life. It transcends age, culture, and circumstance, often creeping into our lives unexpectedly. Yet, amidst this universal experience, art emerges as a powerful antidote, offering solace, connection, and a profound sense of belonging. Through both creation and appreciation, art has the remarkable ability to alleviate feelings of isolation, reminding us that we are never truly alone.

The Universality of Loneliness

Loneliness is not confined to a specific demographic; it affects both young and old. Recent studies have highlighted a surprising trend: young adults are experiencing loneliness at unprecedented rates. A web-based survey revealed that 40% of individuals aged 16 to 24 reported feelings of loneliness, surpassing the 27% reported by those over 75. This challenges the traditional notion that loneliness predominantly affects the elderly.

Several factors contribute to this phenomenon among young adults. The rise of social media, while ostensibly connecting us, often leads to superficial interactions, lacking the depth of genuine relationships. The transitionary nature of young adulthood—navigating careers, education, and personal identities—can also lead to feelings of disconnection.

Conversely, older adults face their own set of challenges. In 2023, one in three adults aged 50–80 reported feeling isolated, a notable increase from previous years. Factors such as retirement, loss of loved ones, and health issues can contribute to this sense of isolation.

Art as a Bridge to Connection

Art, in its myriad forms, serves as a bridge between individuals, fostering connection and understanding. Whether through painting, music, dance, or literature, engaging with art allows us to express emotions that might otherwise remain unspoken. This expression can be both personal and communal, creating opportunities for shared experiences.

Participating in group art activities has been shown to reduce feelings of loneliness and hopelessness, particularly among older adults. A study on clay-based group art therapy found significant decreases in loneliness levels among participants, highlighting the therapeutic potential of communal creative endeavours.

For young adults, art offers a medium to navigate the complexities of identity and belonging. Engaging in creative processes provides an outlet for self-expression, allowing individuals to connect with others who share similar experiences and emotions. This shared understanding fosters a sense of community, mitigating feelings of isolation.

The Neuroscience of Art and Social Connection

The impact of art on loneliness is not solely psychological; it extends to our neurobiology. Engaging in creative activities has been linked to decreased levels of cortisol, the stress hormone, and increased production of dopamine, associated with pleasure and reward. Notably, the brain regions activated during artistic creation overlap with those involved in forming social connections. This neural overlap suggests that art can simulate the experience of social interaction, thereby alleviating feelings of loneliness.

Furthermore, the arts elevate empathy, compassion, and connection on an individual level. They engage our hearts, minds, and souls, fostering a deeper understanding of ourselves and others. This emotional engagement can lead to a heightened sense of belonging and reduced feelings of isolation.

Art Therapy: A Sanctuary for the Lonely

Art therapy has emerged as a sanctuary for those seeking solace from loneliness. It provides a safe space for individuals to explore their emotions, build self-confidence, and foster a sense of community. By engaging in creative processes, individuals can connect with others, share their experiences, and develop supportive relationships.

Art therapy isn't about creating a perfect piece or mastering technique—it's about expression, exploration, and emotional release. I always tell my friends who hesitate to try art that it's not about drawing perfect shapes or making a realistic landscape. It's about self-expression. When they visit, I often hand them a canvas and some paint and just tell them to go for it. No rules, no expectations—just paint. The moment they stop overthinking and start moving the brush, something shifts. It's like they access a part of themselves they didn't even realise needed a voice. I've seen how colours, textures, and even chaotic brush strokes can reveal emotions that words fail to express. Art therapy is not passive; it's an active form of healing that lets you reconnect with yourself. Each stroke, each colour choice, becomes a reflection of what's inside, helping to release emotions, quiet the noise in the mind, and bring a sense of calm.

Beyond just an emotional outlet, I've seen how art helps with loneliness and self-confidence. Even when creating alone, there's a sense of connection—to oneself, to emotions, to something bigger. It's a dialogue between the conscious and the subconscious, a way to make sense of thoughts that feel too tangled to put into words. And when I paint with others, I notice how it creates an unspoken bond. We don't even need to talk— just sitting together, each working on our own canvas, is enough. I've seen friends who were hesitant at first suddenly light up when they step back and look at what they've created. There's a shift, a quiet sense of pride. It's not about talent, but about the act of creating something that didn't exist before. That moment of realisation—of seeing their own creativity take shape—builds confidence in a way few other things can. Over time, it strips away the fear of judgment, making space for self-trust and expression in a way that extends far beyond the canvas.

Group art therapy has been effective in building a sense of community and belonging. Sharing artwork and personal stories with others who have similar experiences fosters empathy, support, and a sense of connection.

Art in the Digital Age: Virtual Communities and Creative Expression

In today's digital landscape, art continues to serve as a unifying force, transcending geographical boundaries. Online platforms and virtual communities have emerged, allowing individuals to share their creative works, participate in collaborative projects, and engage in discussions about art. These digital spaces provide opportunities for connection, particularly for those who may feel isolated in their physical environments.

For instance, virtual art workshops and collaborative online projects enable individuals to engage in creative activities without the constraints of location. Social media platforms dedicated to art allow artists and enthusiasts to share their work, receive feedback, and connect with like-minded individuals. These virtual interactions can foster a sense of community and belonging, mitigating feelings of loneliness.

Personal Reflections: Art as a Lifeline

Reflecting on my own journey, art has been a steadfast companion during moments of solitude. The act of creation provides a sense of purpose and fulfilment, transforming loneliness into a productive and enriching experience. Through art, I have connected with others, shared stories, and built friendships that transcend the canvas.

Art has taught me that solitude does not equate to loneliness. Instead, it offers an opportunity for introspection, growth, and creative exploration. In the quiet moments of creation, I find a deep connection to myself and, paradoxically, to others who share in the human experience.

Loneliness is a multifaceted emotion that affects individuals across all stages of life. However, art offers a powerful remedy, providing avenues for expression, connection, and community. Whether through creating or appreciating art, individuals can find solace and companionship, reminding us that we are never truly alone.

By embracing art, we open ourselves to new experiences, relationships, and a deeper understanding of the human condition. In doing so, we combat loneliness not through avoidance, but through meaningful engagement with the world around us. Art becomes not just a pastime, but a lifeline—a testament to our innate desire for connection and our capacity to find beauty in shared experiences.

Art offers a sense of companionship. Even when alone, the act of creating connects us to something larger.

EXERCISES

1. **Collaborative Art Exchange** – Start a piece and give it to a friend to add onto, creating a shared visual conversation.
2. **Self-Expression Without Words** – Draw something that conveys your emotions without using any recognisable figures or objects.
3. **Letter to Yourself in Art** – Create a visual representation of advice or encouragement you would give your future self.

ART FOR MENTAL HEALTH AND EMOTIONAL INTELLIGENCE

Life has a way of throwing unexpected challenges at us, both personally and professionally. There have been times when I have felt overwhelmed, burdened by the weight of responsibilities, struggling to navigate the turbulence of business and personal life. For an introvert, managing these ups and downs isn't easy. I have always been an overthinker, someone who kept emotions bottled up, unable—or perhaps unwilling—to express them. It took me years to realise how much this internal suppression was affecting not just my mental health but also my interactions with others. It wasn't until I started embracing my artistic side that I discovered a way to process emotions without words.

Art, in its purest form, became my release. Not because I was seeking therapy or looking for a structured way to address stress, but simply because sketching, scribbling, or creating something gave me a moment of quiet clarity. I don't know whether I have ever been clinically anxious or depressed because I never sought medical confirmation. But I do know that I have experienced deep stress, moments of emotional exhaustion, and phases where life felt like a cycle of endless pressure. Art didn't erase these struggles, but it gave me a way to navigate them. It gave me power to pass through those hurdles and come out with clarity.

Art as a Mental Health Anchor

There's an undeniable connection between creativity and mental well-being. Scientific research has shown that engaging in creative activities can reduce symptoms of anxiety, depression, and stress. When immersed in the process of creation, the mind shifts its focus away from overwhelming thoughts, allowing a moment of detachment from stressors. Physiologically, creating art can reduce cortisol levels—the hormone responsible for stress—while simultaneously increasing dopamine, the brain's natural reward chemical.

For me, the impact was subtle at first. Picking up a pencil and sketching random lines didn't feel like a breakthrough. But over time, I noticed something interesting: whenever I engaged in creative work, I felt lighter. It wasn't about the quality of what I produced; it was about the act itself. The process of creating gave me space to think without overthinking, to express without speaking, and to find calm amidst chaos.

Emotional Intelligence Through Art

Beyond mental health, I've realised that art also plays a significant role in emotional intelligence. Emotional intelligence isn't just about understanding emotions; it's about regulating them, responding to them appropriately, and developing self-awareness. I have always been someone who maintained control over my emotions. I rarely expressed them openly, believing that suppression was a form of strength. But the more I immersed myself in art, the more I saw a shift—not just in how I felt but in how I processed emotions.

The Science Behind Creativity and Emotion Regulation

From a scientific perspective, art activates brain regions responsible for emotional processing and self-reflection. Studies have shown that creative activities stimulate the prefrontal cortex, which is responsible for decision-making, emotional regulation, and self-awareness. Engaging in artistic expression has been linked to increased activity in the brain's default mode network—the part of the brain involved in introspection and personal meaning-making.

In simpler terms, when we create, we are not just producing art; we are training our minds to process emotions more effectively. Art provides a safe space to explore difficult feelings, offering an alternative to verbal expression. This is why art therapy has been so effective in treating trauma, grief, and emotional distress.

The Lifelong Impact of Creative Engagement

I don't believe that art solves everything. It doesn't eliminate challenges, nor does it replace the need for other forms of self-care or support. But what it does offer is a pathway—a way to navigate emotions, reduce stress, and build resilience. It is a tool, a sanctuary, a form of quiet resistance against the pressures of life.

For anyone struggling with emotional overwhelm, I would say this: you don't need to be an artist to benefit from art. You don't need skill, technique, or a polished final product. You just need a willingness to engage with it. Whether it's sketching, painting, writing, or even doodling absentmindedly on a scrap of paper—each act of creation is an act of self-care.

Art has given me more than an outlet. It has given me a way to listen to myself, to understand my own emotions without fear of judgment. It has helped me transition from someone who bottled everything up to someone who sees the value in expression. In that sense, art is not just a creative pursuit; it is a practice in self-awareness, a quiet yet powerful force for emotional and mental well-being.

Art has therapeutic qualities that enhance emotional well-being and self-awareness.

EXERCISES

1. **Emotion to Art** – Assign a colour and shape to your current mood, translating feelings into visual form.
2. **Non-Dominant Hand Drawing** – Use your non-dominant hand to draw freely, letting go of control.
3. **Affirmation Art** – Choose a personal affirmation and create an artwork around it.

Art - It is a mind-set, a way of thinking, seeing, meditating, focusing, learning, expressing, and a way of being yourself. Art is not limited to painting or drawing—it can take any form of expression or creation, whether through music, writing, design, problem-solving, or even the way we navigate challenges in life and work. As explored throughout this book, the principles that guide artistic expression also shape leadership, business, and personal growth. Whether through letting go of control, embracing uncertainty, or using art as a tool for idea generation, the act of creating teaches us patience, adaptability, and the courage to explore new perspectives. But beyond technique and creativity, being an artist—in any form—is about adopting a mind-set that helps us grow, innovate, and navigate life with more clarity and intent.

When we begin to see art as more than just an act of creation—as a way of understanding the world and ourselves—we unlock its power in every aspect of life. That mind-set makes us better leaders, sharper decision-makers, and more open, resilient individuals. The lessons are always there—it's just up to us to recognise them, embrace them, and bring them into our daily lives. Just like an artist approaches a blank canvas with curiosity and intent, we, too, can shape our experiences with the same boldness and vision. The canvas of life is ours to paint—how we choose to fill it is entirely up to us.